Practicing Basic

Spiritual Disciplines

By

Charles F. Stanley

Thomas Nelson
Since 1798

Published in Nashville, Tennessee, by Thomas Nelson, Inc., Publishers, and distributed in Canada by Word Communications, Ltd., Richmond, British Columbia.

Editing, layout, and design by Gregory C. Benoit Publishing, Old Mystic, CT

ISBN 9781418541170

Printed in the United States of America

09 10 11 12 wc 7 6 5 4 3

Contents

Our Blueprint for Strength

Every building begins with a blueprint. If the engineering is faulty on the blueprint, the resulting structure will be weak. The same is true for our spiritual life. The strength of our spiritual life rests first and foremost on the absolute, utter reliability and truth of God's Word. Thank God that we have a blueprint for spiritual strength that does not fail!

The Bible is a blueprint on which we can rely with absolute confidence. The Bible gives us God's truth, and it also tells us how to apply God's truth to our daily lives. It is a book of genuine wisdom about how to become strong and stay strong spiritually. It is the reference to which we must return continually to make certain that we are staying on track in our spiritual growth.

Builders return to blueprints often during the construction of a structure, and so we also must return to the Bible often during the development of our spiritual lives and the spiritual growth of our church.

This book can be used by you alone or by several people in a small-group study. At various times, you will be asked to relate to the material in one of these four ways:

1. *What new insights have you gained?* Make notes about the insights that you have. You may want to record them in your Bible or in a separate journal. As you reflect back over your insights, you are likely to see how God has moved in your life.

2. *Have you ever had a similar experience?* Each of us approaches the Bible from a unique background—our own particular set of relationships and experiences. Our experiences do not make the Bible true—the Word of God is truth regardless of our opinion about it. It is important, however, to share our experiences in order to see how God's truth can be applied to human lives.

3. *How do you feel about the material presented?* Emotional responses do not give validity to the Scriptures, nor should we trust our emotions as a gauge for our faith. In small-group Bible study, however, it is good for participants to express their emotions. The Holy Spirit often communicates with us through this unspoken language.

4. *In what way do you feel challenged to respond or to act?* God's Word may cause you to feel inspired or challenged to change something in your life. Take the challenge seriously and find ways of acting upon it. If God reveals to you a particular need that He wants *you* to address, take that as "marching orders" from God. God is expecting you to *do* something with the challenge that He has just given you.

Start and conclude your Bible study sessions in prayer. Ask God to give you spiritual eyes to see and spiritual ears to hear. As you conclude your study, ask the Lord to seal what you have learned so that you will never forget it. Ask Him to help you grow into the fullness of the stature of Christ Jesus.

Again, I caution you to keep the Bible at the center of your study. A genuine Bible study stays focused on God's Word and promotes a growing faith and a closer walk with the Holy Spirit in *each* person who participates.

The Strength of the Believer

LEARNING: WHAT DOES IT MEAN TO BE SPIRITUALLY STRONG?

GROWING: HOW CAN I REMAIN CONSISTENTLY STRONG?

Of one thing we can be certain today: the Lord wants our faith as Christians to be rock-solid. At no time do we find the Lord calling His people to be weak in spiritual power, wavering in purpose, or wandering aimlessly through life. We are called to be strong in faith, certain of our salvation, and sure of our direction and eternal destiny.

The Bible describes the Lord as a rock. David said this in a praise song to the Lord:

I will love You, O LORD, my strength.
The LORD is my rock and my fortress and my deliverer;
My God, my strength, in whom I will trust.

—Psalm 18:1–2

3

Elsewhere in the Psalms David referred to the Lord as the rock of his strength, the rock of his salvation, and the rock of his refuge (Ps. 62:7; 89:26; 94:22). The Lord was his sure foundation, an immovable, impenetrable fortress. In the New Testament we find Jesus referred to as our spiritual Rock (1 Cor. 10:4). He is the chief cornerstone on which the entire church has been built (Eph. 2:20).

When we trust Jesus Christ to be our Savior and Lord, we are placing ourselves on the sure, firm foundation that never falters and never fails. We are placing ourselves on a foundation that does not shift, crumble, or crack. We are placing ourselves on a foundation that is eternal and unchanging. We are part of God's holy and living temple—a "dwelling place of God in the Spirit"—and as such we are to bear the same qualities as the foundation on which we are built (Eph. 2:21–22). We are to remain strong in times of crisis or persecution, solid in our understanding of the Scriptures, sure of our relationship with the Lord, and steadfast in our pursuit of all that the Holy Spirit calls us to. God's people are to be like boulders in a world of shifting sands.

Though the world says that black is white and white is black, that morals don't matter, and that all things are relative, we are to stand strong as Christians, clearly discerning right from wrong, good from bad, and the eternal from the temporary. The world calls us to do what feels good and justifies behavior under the banner of "everybody is doing it," but we are to stand strong as Christians and declare that our behavior is rooted in our faith, not our emotions. Even if everybody around us bows to the false gods of this age, we will not bow.

While the world calls us to reject God's commandments as old-fashioned or out of touch, we are to stand strong as Christians and declare that God changes not; His commandments are as applicable today as they were in Bible times, and God is always in touch with the human heart and human need. The world calls us to do what is politically correct, economically expedient, and morally compromising, but we are to stand strong as Christians and choose to be God's people, generous in helping the needy, pure in our hearts, and uncompromising in our belief that God is sovereign.

The Prerequisites for Godly Strength

Any athlete knows he must do certain things to become strong. He must eat foods that build up his body physically; he must exercise in ways that produce strength, flexibility, and endurance; and he must get sufficient rest for the renewal of his muscles. There is a *discipline* required of those who desire to become good athletes. The higher the level of performance the athlete seeks, the greater the discipline required to reach it.

The same is true for us in our spiritual walk. If we are going to be strong in the faith, we must follow a spiritual discipline. We must take into our lives those things that produce strength in us and eliminate those things that result in weakness, laziness, or spiritual compromise. We must exercise our spiritual muscles by using our faith in ways that promote the spread of the gospel, strengthen the body of Christ, and meet the physical and spiritual needs we encounter. We must learn to rest in the Lord, trusting Him always to provide for us and protect us against the enemy of our souls.

The Christian life cannot be lived on a whim, following fad beliefs. It must be a life of consistent, daily discipline. The apostle Paul challenged the Philippians, "Let your conduct be worthy of the gospel of Christ" (Phil. 1:27). That is always our goal.

A Life of Consistency

As a pastor, I have asked countless people, "How are you doing?" and I have received these replies: "Oh, I'm having my ups and downs;" "Well, I'm going through a wilderness time right now;" and "I'm trying to stay on top of things."

Some have admitted to me: "I'm not as close to the Lord as I should be;" or "I've been away from the Lord but I'm on my way back;" or "I'm dry right now."

These statements all suggest that most Christians do not live the *consistently strong* spiritual life they desire and know God wants them to live. They are riding the roller coaster of life, rather than walking a steady, upward path. When I have asked, "What are you doing to be strong spiritually?" I have heard a variety of answers, but I often receive a response that means, "I don't know what to do." Many have never imagined that it is possible to live a *consistently strong* spiritual life. They take ups and downs for granted and even expect them.

That is not what the Lord desires for us. Paul said to the Colossians, "I am with you in spirit, rejoicing to see your good order and the steadfastness of your faith in Christ. As you therefore have received Christ Jesus the Lord, so walk in Him, rooted and built up in Him and established in the faith, as you have been taught, abounding in it with thanksgiving" (Col. 2:5–7). He assured the Colossians that they would be "holy, and blameless, and above reproach" if they would "continue in the faith, grounded and steadfast, and [not be] moved away from the hope of the gospel" (Col. 1:22–23). Paul wrote to the Ephesians, "Be strong in the Lord and in the power of His might" (Eph. 6:10).

What must we do to be strong and to remain strong in spirit? How are we to discipline our lives to be consistent and unwavering in our walk of faith? The elements of our disciplined life in Christ are the subject of this Bible study. As you read through these lessons, let me encourage you on these three points:

First, the foundation of spiritual discipline is the same whether we are newborn babes in Christ—the newly saved—or longtime Christians. We never outgrow our need for the basics of spiritual discipline. We never outgrow our need for God's Word, our need to pray, God's command to give, our need for Christian fellowship, or God's call to ministry. No person is so spiritually mature that he or she can ignore the basics and still remain strong over time.

Second, the foundation of spiritual discipline is the same regardless of our personal circumstances. Pastors and laymen need to pursue the same basic spiritual disciplines to be strong in the Lord. Everyone— men and women, rich and poor, young and old, highly educated and uneducated—needs the same basic spiritual discipline.

Third, the spiritual discipline that calls us to pursue God's Word is one that we can each pursue. I once met a person who said to me, "I'm just not as spiritual as some people. I struggle more." The fact is, we all struggle to remain consistent in our spiritual lives. The fact is also this: God has given each of us the will necessary to pursue a disciplined spiritual life and also the power of the Holy Spirit to help us remain strong and consistent in our spiritual walk. Our will plus the Holy Spirit's power is true *willpower*. Every person *can* become spiritually disciplined.

☙ Would you classify yourself as a weak or strong Christian?

☙ What are you doing with regularity in order to remain consistently spiritually strong?

☙ In what areas have you struggled to remain consistently strong in your faith?

☙ Today and Tomorrow ☙

TODAY: THE LORD GIVES ME HIS HOLY SPIRIT'S POWER TO ENABLE ME TO BE STRONG.

TOMORROW: I WILL SPEND TIME THIS WEEK WORKING ON REGULAR SPIRITUAL DISCIPLINES.

LESSON 2

Obedience to God's Commandments

─────── ✎ **In This Lesson** ✍ ───────

LEARNING: WHAT IS THE MOST IMPORTANT SPIRITUAL DISCIPLINE?

GROWING: HOW CAN I KNOW WHAT I'M SUPPOSED TO DO?

∽∾

Obedience is not a popular word in today's culture. A person will be much more readily accepted by the world at large if he is tolerant, compromising, lenient, or "relational"—seeing all things as relevant and doing one's best to keep everybody happy and satisfied at all costs. God's Word calls us to be obedient to all of God's laws, statutes, and commandments, which is often counter-cultural. There can be no spiritual growth—no genuine spiritual power or effective ministry to the lost—without obedience. A rebellious heart is contrary to spiritual strength.

Rebellion is the foremost reason for a lack of spiritual authority, a lack of intimacy with God, and a lack of genuine blessings and rewards from God's hand. When many of us think of rebels, we think of juvenile delinquents, criminals, or those who are opposed to the establishment or the current political order. The Bible defines *rebellion* in a much different way; it refers to *any* person as rebellious who enacts his own set of standards or does his own thing, contrary to the commandments of God. Those who willfully choose their way over God's way are rebels.

⚘ In what ways have you struggled with rebellion in the past, choosing your way over God's way?

> For rebellion is as the sin of witchcraft, and stubbornness is as iniquity and idolatry.
>
> —1 Samuel 15:23

⚘ Why does God say that a rebellious spirit is the same as the sin of witchcraft?

⤙ In what ways is stubbornness the same as idolatry?

The Heart of Our Relationship with God

As completely as the Lord stands against rebellion, He supports and upholds those who are obedient. Obedience to God's commandments is highly praised by God in the Bible. It is "better than sacrifice" in His eyes (1 Sam. 15:22). At the very heart of our relationship with God lies obedience to God's commandments—an adherence to doing things *God's* way and a submission to seeking *God's* plan for our lives.

Even our salvation is an expression of obedience. We are not in a position to devise our own means of salvation or to choose the method, timetable, or related circumstances for our salvation. We must accept *God's* plan for our salvation and obey what God requires of us to receive His forgiveness of sins and eternal life. We must believe in Jesus Christ as the one complete sacrifice for our sin, receive His Holy Spirit into our lives, and willingly obey Him as our Lord. As the writer to the Hebrews said,

Though He [Jesus] was a Son, yet He learned obedience by the things which He suffered. And having been perfected, He became the author of eternal salvation to all who obey Him.

—Hebrews 5:8–9

None of us is in a position to require God to do things our way or to forgive us according to any plan that we might present to Him. All of us are required by God to do things His way and to willingly submit ourselves to His plan for forgiveness and salvation.

When I was young, my grandfather said to me, "Charles, if God tells you to run at a brick wall, then you run at that brick wall with all your strength, trusting Him to open the way for you." There simply is no substitute for obedience if we desire to see the full manifestation of God's trustworthiness, presence, and power in our lives. Obedience is the key to our having a truly intimate relationship with God. And having such a relationship with God is what spiritual discipline is all about! The very goal of all spiritual disciplines is knowing God more intimately and experiencing more of Him at work in us and through us.

Has the LORD as great delight in burnt offerings and sacrifices, as in obeying the voice of the LORD? Behold, to obey is better than sacrifice, and to heed than the fat of rams.

—1 Samuel 15:22

🔊 When have you tried to appease the Lord by sacrificing something while disobeying His word in another area? What was the result?

🔊 In what area might the Lord be calling you to stricter obedience this week?

The Hindrance of Sin

Sin might be considered another word for acts of willful disobedience, and it always has negative consequences. Ultimately, a state of sinfulness brings about a person's spiritual death (Rom. 6:23). But even in the life of the believer who has turned to the Lord and received His forgiveness, sin exists and has consequences. It is a tremendous hindrance to the work that the Lord desires to do.

The writer to the Hebrews said,

> Therefore we also, since we are surrounded by so great a cloud of witnesses, let us lay aside every weight, and the sin which so easily ensnares us, and let us run with endurance the race that is set before us.

> —Hebrews 12:1

Sin is a weight and a snare. It slows us down, trips us up, and at times delays or detours us from fulfilling God's purposes and plans. Part of our obedience to the Lord is to ask the Lord to forgive us *daily* for those things that we have thought, said, or done that are contrary to His commandments. That is the only way we can avoid chastening from the Lord. It is the only way we can experience the fullness of God's blessings.

☙ How can sin be like a runner carrying lead weights on his back? What is involved in "laying aside" those weights?

What "race" is set before you? What might be hindering you in that race at present?

A Passion to Obey

There are several benchmarks by which we can evaluate if we are obeying God and developing spiritual discipline:

1. Obedience as Our Bottom Line

Obedience to God must become the bottom line of every decision we make. The obedient person sifts every decision through the will of God, asking, "Can I do this and be obedient to God and His commandments and plan for my life?" Even in those situations in which we feel inadequate and find ourselves struggling with fear, suffering, loss, or painful consequences, our desire must be to obey God's will.

2. Instant Obedience

When the Holy Spirit speaks to an obedient person's heart, that person doesn't even stop to consider whether he will act. He responds instantly.

3. A Yearning for the Heart and Mind of God

The obedient Christian desires to learn more and more about how God works and what He desires. He has a deep yearning to seek the mind of God and to know God better. We certainly will never learn all there is to know about God—we will never know Him with total intimacy. But our desire must be to know Him better and better. For us to grow spiritually, we must continually ask, "What is it that God truly desires for my life? How does God want me to act? What does He want me to say?"

Our role is not to take our plans to God and ask Him to bless them. Our role is to ask God what He wants us to do with our lives—our time, our talents, and our material substance—and then do His bidding.

4. God's Opinion Is All That Matters

To the truly obedient Christian, the opinions of others are never more important than the opinion of God. The obedient person has no concern about whether others may reject or ridicule him. The only acceptance that truly counts is God's acceptance. The obedient person may seek out the counsel of godly people, but he does not act on human consensus. He does what God requires even if all counsel is against God's command.

5. Willing to Accept Consequences of Obedience

The obedient person is willing to accept adverse consequences of his obedience. He is willing to suffer for Christ's sake—not eager to suffer, but joyful in the midst of suffering. As Jesus taught, "Blessed are those who are persecuted for righteousness' sake, for theirs is the kingdom of heaven" (Matt. 5:10).

For none of us lives to himself, and no one dies to himself. For if we live, we live to the Lord; and if we die, we die to the Lord. Therefore, whether we live or die, we are the Lord's.

—Romans 14:7–8

🖝 What does it mean to "live to the Lord"? To "die to the Lord"?

🖝 How well does your life reflect Paul's priorities in these verses? Consider your time, money, energy, and relationships.

The Rewards of Obedience

There are a number of consequences of being obedient to God's Word, and not all of them are positive. Every person who lives in obedience to the Lord will suffer to a certain degree because he is going against the grain of the world. The positive rewards from God, however, far outweigh anything that the world might do to the believer:

A growing faith. The obedient person sees God's faithfulness in action and grows in faith as a result.

Blessings. God bestows His blessings upon those who are obedient, not only spiritual blessings but financial, material, and relational blessings.

An enlarged view of God. The person who is obedient moves into a more intimate relationship with God. The closer we come to God, the more we experience His love and the more we are able to see His omnipotence and omniscience (His infinite and absolute power and wisdom). Those who are obedient grow in reverence for God and have an increased sense of security in God's deep and abiding love.

A greater effectiveness in witnessing. Others around us will see our obedience—family members, friends, coworkers, fellow church members, lost souls—and they will be affected by our steadfast faithfulness to God's commands. They can't help being influenced in a positive way toward the gospel, regardless of what they may claim.

Greater ability to discern the Holy Spirit at work in our lives. Those who are obedient hear the Holy Spirit with greater clarity and have greater recognition of His voice. They are able to discern with accuracy what the Holy Spirit directs them to do and to discern when and how to act.

Whether it is pleasing or displeasing, we will obey the voice of the LORD our God to whom we send you, that it may be well with us when we obey the voice of the LORD our God.

—Jeremiah 42:6

When have you obeyed the Lord's commands even though it seemed unpleasant? What was the result?

When have you seen someone else obeying the Lord at great cost to himself? How did that person's obedience influence you?

Obedience is truly the bottom line for all spiritual discipline. Everything else that we *do* that builds spiritual discipline is established on a foundation of obedience. We pray, for example, in obedience to God's command to pray. We read God's Scriptures because we desire to know God's statutes and obey them and also because we are commanded to study the Word. Our quest to know the Lord is rooted in obedience at all times. Obedience is not the ultimate motivation for spiritual discipline—a love for God, a longing to know Him, and faith in Him are the true motives for the mature believer—but obedience is required if we are to grow spiritually and experience more and more of God's love.

For though we walk in the flesh, we do not war according to the flesh. For the weapons of our warfare are not carnal but mighty in God for pulling down strongholds.

—2 Corinthians 10:3–4

☙ What war is the Christian engaged in? What are the weapons that we wield?

What role does obedience to God's Word play in this warfare? What effect does disobedience have?

Today and Tomorrow

TODAY: THE LORD WANTS ME TO DEVELOP OBEDIENCE ABOVE ALL OTHER DISCIPLINES.

TOMORROW: THIS WEEK I WILL ASK THE LORD TO SHOW ME AREAS OF MY LIFE WHERE I NEED TO OBEY HIM MORE.

❦ Notes and Prayer Requests: ❦

LESSON 3

Conformity to Christ

─────────── ❧ In This Lesson ☙ ───────────

LEARNING: WHAT DOES IT MEAN TO BE CONFORMED TO CHRIST?

GROWING: HOW IS THIS DONE?

∽∞∾

Do you have a spiritual goal today? Without a goal we rarely achieve all that we can achieve. That is true in the spiritual realm just as much as it is true in the worlds of business and personal finance, family life, education, or physical fitness.

The goal for every Christian is clearly stated by the apostle Paul in his letter to the Romans:

> And we know that all things work together for good to those who love God, to those who are the called according to His purpose. For whom He foreknew, He also predestined to be conformed to the image of His Son, that He might be the first-born among many brethren. Moreover whom He predestined, these He also called; whom He called, these He also justified; and whom He justified, these He also glorified.
>
> —Romans 8:28–30

What things does God work together to produce good in a Christian's life? What things are beyond His scope of influence, according to these verses?

If God works *all* things together for good, what does that mean regarding the present circumstances in your life? Regarding the future? Regarding the past?

The Conformity Process

I want to call your attention specifically to three key truths in this passage from Romans 8:28–30. These truths are important for you as you practice basic spiritual disciplines and grow in Christ.

1. Destined to Be Conformed

From the beginning God has chosen you to be His beloved child and to be conformed to the image of Christ. "To be conformed" implies that, at present, a person is *not* conformed to Christ's image, and we certainly know that's true for each one of us. None of us has lived a sinless life; not one of us is without fault. All of us have imperfect backgrounds and had imperfect childhoods and experiences that have left us wounded and scarred, and all of us need healing in some area. No matter how mature we are in our walk with the Lord, there is *more* that must be changed in us for us to be *fully* like Christ Jesus. Only the Lord can say, "I change not," because only the Lord can say, "I do not need change." Every one of us can look in the mirror and say, "Lord, change me in the ways that I need to be changed."

> But we all, with unveiled face, beholding as in a mirror the glory of the Lord, are being transformed into the same image from glory to glory, just as by the Spirit of the Lord.
>
> —2 Corinthians 3:18

⤙ In what ways does God transform a person to become more like Christ?

☙ What is God's role in this process? What is your role?

2. Conformed to Christ's Image

To be conformed to Christ's image means that a person is an accurate and total reflection of Christ. In other words, when others look at us, they do not see anything in what we say and do that is *contrary* to what Jesus would have said and done if He were on earth in fleshly form today. A person who is *completely* conformed to Christ's image would think, speak, and act exactly as Christ would think, speak, and act in any situation.

Again, we know this is not true for any person. We all have sinned and continue to sin, even though we have no desire to sin. We are imperfect, finite, fleshly creatures. Nevertheless, we are called by God to grow in our likeness of Christ until that day when God fully perfects us and we put on the full image of Christ Jesus.

Do not lie to one another, since you have put off the old man with his deeds, and have put on the new man who is renewed in knowledge according to the image of Him who created him.

—Colossians 3:9–10

🖎 Who or what is the "old man" that Paul refers to here? Who is the "new man"?

🖎 What is involved in "putting off" the old man and "putting on" the new?

27

3. God's Work, Not Ours

Paul never told the Romans they were to strive to be perfect or conformed to Christ. He said that this would be the work of the Holy Spirit in them. Look again at Romans 8:28–30 on the first page of this chapter and circle each *He* that you find in that passage. It is God who does the foreknowing, the predestining, the conforming, the calling, the justifying, and the glorifying. The conforming work in us is not something for which we are totally responsible. We are to live by faith and obey, and then trust God to do a transforming work in us.

Circle each instance of "He" in Romans 8:28–30 on page 23. List below what things God accomplishes.

What part do you play in those processes? What part does God play?

Our Ultimate Purpose in Life

A Christian should never have a doubt about what he is to do in this life, about what goals he should set or what pursuits he should follow. Our ultimate goal in life is to do those things that conform us to Christ's image. Nothing else that we do will have the same eternal reward as the pursuit of Christ.

Developing the Mind of Christ

Most of us have seen the bracelets and bumper stickers that say "WWJD," meaning "What Would Jesus Do?" While that is a wonderful message, it is far from complete. We are not only to do what Jesus would *do*; we are also to say what He would say, think what He thinks, and believe what He believes.

The apostle Paul very specifically taught whom we are to be conformed to and what we are not to be conformed to:

> And do not be conformed to this world, but be transformed by the renewing of your mind, that you may prove what is that good and acceptable and perfect will of God.

—Romans 12:2

What does it mean to be "conformed to this world"? Give some specific examples.

∼ What does it mean to renew your mind? How is this done?

To have the mind of Christ is to:

∼ *Have a desire to serve others.* The person who thinks as Jesus thinks has an automatic impulse to help others in need. He doesn't even stop to think about whether he should help a person who is in trouble. He moves immediately to that person's side to offer whatever assistance he can give, both practical and spiritual.

∼ *Have a perfect understanding of right and wrong.* The person who thinks like Jesus has righteous and pure thoughts. He knows God's absolutes and God's desires for good. He doesn't have to contemplate whether an activity or thought is "right:" he knows immediately whether something lines up with God's commandments and God's nature. He has the ability to discern a lie from the truth and to know whether a thought is a temptation from the enemy or a directive from the Holy Spirit.

᙭ *Clearly discern spiritual matters*. The person who thinks like Jesus is strongly rooted in obedience to God's commandments and knows the nature of God, so he is able to discern clearly between false and true doctrines. He is able to judge the biblical authenticity of spiritual manifestations. He knows how to judge the spirits and to determine if something is from God.

᙭ *Make wise decisions and choices*. The person who thinks like Jesus knows how to make godly decisions, including how to choose friends and coworkers.

We do not have the mind of Christ instantly upon our conversion. Just as a newborn baby grows in his ability to understand the world, so the newborn Christian must grow in his understanding of God's nature, God's commandments, and the fullness of God's Word. Furthermore, the will of a person is always involved. You must *want* to develop the mind of Christ. You must *seek* to know God's Word so that you can find God's answers, direction, and solutions. You must *ask* God to impart His wisdom to you.

Conformity Through Suffering

There is another aspect to our being conformed to Christ that many Christians do not like to face: suffering. The Christian life is not immune to suffering. In fact, in many ways the call of Christ is a call to suffer. It is a call to identify with those who are hurting, which always requires a sacrifice of self and laying aside one's pride. The call of Christ is also a call to be willing to experience the persecution of the world and to suffer rejection. We *identify* with Christ in our sufferings, for He, too, suffered and aligned Himself with those who suffered.

The most fertile time of spiritual growth for most Christians comes during a time of suffering—of crisis, illness, persecution, loss, pain, rejection. Suffering is the means God often uses to perfect us and to create in us the true character of Christ. I challenge you not to shy away from difficulties or troublesome people but to see them as opportunities to minister the love of Christ.

> Therefore, since Christ suffered for us in the flesh, arm yourselves also with the same mind, for he who has suffered in the flesh has ceased from sin, that he no longer should live the rest of his time in the flesh for the lusts of men, but for the will of God.

—1 Peter 4:1–2

How does a Christian arm himself with the mind of Christ? How is the mind of Christ different from the mind of man?

In what ways does suffering help to purge us from sin? What is required of us for this to happen?

 Today and Tomorrow

TODAY: GOD WANTS ME TO BECOME MORE AND MORE LIKE HIS SON.

TOMORROW: I WILL ASK THE LORD THIS WEEK TO SHOW ME WAYS THAT I CAN IMITATE JESUS.

∽ **Notes and Prayer Requests:** ∽

LESSON 4

A Personal Study of the Scriptures

—— ⚘ **In This Lesson** ⚘ ——

LEARNING: WHERE DOES THE BIBLE COME INTO THIS PROCESS?

GROWING: HOW CAN I HOPE TO UNDERSTAND WHAT THE BIBLE TEACHES?

A person must know God's Word if he or she is to develop the mind of Christ, move into obedience to God's commandments, and become more conformed to Christ. The person who wants to experience more of the presence and power of God must discipline himself to read and study God's Word for himself. There is no substitute for it! Your study of God's Word must be:

⚘ **Personal.** I meet people all the time who admit to me that they take their Bible to church and read along as the pastor reads a passage of Scripture or preaches on it, but they then let their Bible gather dust the rest of the week. Some say, "I listen to teaching tapes about the Bible." Others tell me they read books that are religious or that are about what God says in the Bible.

These are all good things to do, but none of them is a substitute for personal reading and study of God's Word, because knowing God's Word is more than knowing the content of God's Word—its stories, commandments, and teachings. It is knowing how to *apply* God's Word to daily life. We each have different jobs, roles, family affiliations, cultural settings, communities, and churches. We have different needs—physical, financial, relational, emotional, and spiritual. We are at different levels of spiritual maturity. We *must* read and study the Bible for ourselves to allow the Bible to speak to our unique, individual circumstances and relationships.

The primary way God is going to speak to you is through His Word. Certainly God does speak to people through other means, but His *primary* way of speaking to men and women today is through His Word. As you read His Word, ask the Holy Spirit to give you understanding and impart to you the specific knowledge that you need directly from God.

☙ *Daily.* For you continually to grow in the Lord and remain strong in Him, you must read God's Word daily, simply because our lives are lived daily. A part of the Lord's Prayer is, "Give us this day our daily bread" (Matt. 6:11). *Bread* refers not only to physical bread, but also to the spiritual bread we need to feed our souls.

No person eats only once a week; we all eat daily, usually several times a day. What is true for the physical is also true for the spiritual. We need to read the Bible daily to give our minds and hearts the spiritual nutrition they need to face life's daily demands.

We wash our bodies daily, and we must wash our minds daily in God's Word. The Word of God has a cleansing action on us. It convicts us of our daily sins—wrong things we have done and things we should have done—so that we might confess our sins daily and live in a constant state of repentance.

If we confess our sins, He is faithful and just to forgive us our sins and to cleanse us from all unrighteousness. If we say that we have not sinned, we make Him a liar, and His word is not in us.

—1 John 1:9–10

What is involved in being cleansed from sin?

What role does God's Word play in this process?

∽ *Understandable.* Read a version of the Bible that you understand. There is no benefit in reading a version that seems like a foreign language to you. Then, as you read your Bible every day, read it until you gain meaning and understanding. Don't let your mind wander to other things; concentrate on what you are reading. Don't just read the words at the surface. Look for the deeper meaning in the passage. Ask yourself continually, "How does this apply to what I am facing right now? What is God saying to me? What is the deeper meaning of this verse? Why is this passage important for me to read and to remember?"

As you read your Bible daily, look for connections between what you are reading and what you have read previously. Look at the broader context of a passage. Most passages of Scripture are directly connected to those passages immediately preceding and immediately following. Also look for the ways in which a passage might be linked to other passages on the same general theme, both in the Old Testament and New Testament. Look for links between what Jesus said and what Paul taught, John taught, or Peter taught. Look for ways in which Jesus fulfills the teachings of the Old Testament. Look for symbols and key words that are repeated again and again, from cover to cover. The more you make connections between what you read in one place in the Bible and other references, the more you will grow in your understanding of the *whole* of God's Word.

∽ *Prayerful.* As you read the Bible, ask God to reveal Christ to you through the Holy Spirit. Ask Him to show you how He wants you to live. Ask Him to reveal specific guidance for the decisions you are currently facing. Ask the Lord to show you how to apply what you read to your life.

Whom will he teach knowledge? And whom will he make to understand the message? Those just weaned from milk? Those just drawn from the breasts? For precept must be upon precept, precept upon precept, Line upon line, line upon line, Here a little, there a little.

—Isaiah 28:9–10

🖝 What does Isaiah mean when he speaks about learning from "precept upon precept"? How does this apply to daily Bible reading?

🖝 Why does Isaiah contrast those who learn God's precepts versus "those just weaned from milk"? What is required for a Christian to grow to spiritual maturity?

39

The Benefits of Reading the Bible

The more you read your Bible, the greater will be your understanding of God's commandments and goals for your life. You will see more clearly *how* the Lord wants you to live. Specifically, you are going to gain a new or deeper understanding about the call of God on your life in these four areas:

1. A Godly Life

Each of us is called to live a godly life, one that is holy, pure, and righteous. Again and again, we find stories in the Bible that might be described as before and after spiritual makeovers. Again and again, we find God's commands to put off our old nature and put on the character of Christ Jesus. The more you read your Bible, the more you are going to come face-to-face with practical changes God wants you to make in the way that you think, speak, and act. Consider this very applicable passage from Ephesians:

> Therefore, putting away lying, "Let each one of you speak truth with his neighbor," for we are members of one another. "Be angry, and do not sin": do not let the sun go down on your wrath, nor give place to the devil. Let him who stole steal no longer, but rather let him labor, working with his hands what is good, that he may have something to give him who has need. Let no corrupt word proceed out of your mouth, but what is good for necessary edification, that it may impart grace to the hearers ... Let all bitterness, wrath, anger, clamor, and evil speaking be put away from you, with all malice. And be kind to one another, tenderhearted, forgiving one another, even as God in Christ forgave you.
>
> —Ephesians 4:25–29, 31–32

In just a few verses, the apostle Paul gave several specific instructions about what it means to live a godly life. There can be little room for misinterpretation of these verses! God's Word continually challenges us to live exemplary, sinless lives. The Lord wants us to live genuinely good, righteous lives, and He makes it possible for us to live such lives by the power of His Holy Spirit.

∽ Define each of the following in your own words, giving practical examples of each.

Bitterness:

Wrath:

Clamor:

Tenderhearted:

Forgiving:

2. Eternal Purpose

Each of us is called to invest our life in those things that have eternal purpose. From cover to cover the Bible speaks of God's everlasting nature, His desire for us to be with Him for all eternity, and His eternal purposes. The more you read your Bible, the more you will gain an eternal perspective and grow in your understanding that only those things that are linked to Christ Jesus truly last.

You will also gain an understanding that there is no such thing as a "secular job." All jobs exist so that Christ might be manifested through them. God's love, healing, and forgiveness can be made known through all situations. No part of your life is apart from Christ. He desires to touch every aspect of your life with His eternal presence and power. Because of this, your life has tremendous meaning. The greatest satisfaction in life comes in knowing that Christ is in you and is accomplishing His eternal purposes not only in you but through you.

> Therefore do not be unwise, but understand what the will of the Lord is.
>
> —Ephesians 5:17

How does a person "understand what the will of the Lord is"? What is required of you? What is God's role?

⤳ What part does the Bible play in that process?

3. A Role in God's Plan

Each of us is called to a specific role as part of God's greater purpose for all mankind. The more you read your Bible, the more you are going to gain a vision for God's greater purposes and plans for mankind. You are going to see yourself in the context of God's greater will. No longer is the big "I" at the center of the universe; rather, Christ is central. You will gain an understanding that God does not exist for *you*, but rather, you exist for *God*. God doesn't exist to be molded into your purpose, but rather, you were created to be part of His purpose. God's purpose for your life is that you bring glory to Christ Jesus and that, by your witness, the world may come to know Jesus Christ as Savior and Lord.

Jesus challenged His disciples, "Go therefore and make disciples of all the nations, baptizing them in the name of the Father and of the Son and of the Holy Spirit, teaching them to observe all things that I have commanded you; and lo, I am with you always, even to the end of the age" (Matt. 28:19–20). To make disciples, we must be prepared and willing to teach others everything we learn from God's Word. Teaching does not have to be formal; we can teach the truth of God informally in our daily conversations and by being a witness for Christ every time we have an opportunity to share the gospel.

∽ What things has Jesus commanded you? How well are you obeying those commands at present?

∽ How can an untrained Christian "make disciples of all the nations"? In what ways can you be teaching others about God's Word?

4. Victory over Satan

Each of us is called to have victory over the enemy of our souls. The more we read the Bible, the more we learn how to have victory over sin and over the enemy of our souls. We have greater strength to withstand the devil's temptations. When Jesus was tempted by the devil, He did not respond with human wisdom, but by quoting the Word of God. Read again the account of Jesus' temptations and note how He replied to each of them:

Then Jesus was led up by the Spirit into the wilderness to be tempted by the devil. And when He had fasted forty days and forty nights, afterward He was hungry. Now when the tempter came to Him, he said, "If You are the Son of God, command that these stones become bread."

But He answered and said, "It is written, 'Man shall not live by bread alone, but by every word that proceeds from the mouth of God' " [Deut. 8:3].

Then the devil took Him up into the holy city, set Him on the pinnacle of the temple, and said to Him, "If You are the Son of God, throw Yourself down" ...

Jesus said to him, "It is written again, 'You shall not tempt the LORD your God' " [Deut. 6:16].

Again, the devil took Him up on an exceedingly high mountain, and showed Him all the kingdoms of the world and their glory. And he said to Him, "All these things I will give You if You will fall down and worship me."

Then Jesus said to him, "Away with you, Satan! For it is written, 'You shall worship the LORD your God, and Him only you shall serve' " [Deut. 6:13].

Then the devil left Him, and behold, angels came and ministered to Him.

—Matthew 4:1–11

To be able to say boldly to the devil, "It is written," a person must first know *what* is written!

> Your word I have hidden in my heart, that I might not sin against You.

> —Psalm 119:11

☙ What does it mean to hide God's Word in your heart? How is this done? What effect does it have?

☙ How did Jesus' knowledge of Scripture help Him face temptation? When has Scripture knowledge helped you in the past?

Bible Study Yields Specific Direction

How do daily Bible reading and Bible study differ? Bible *study* is an intense search of God's Word to learn more about what God has to say on a particular subject. Very often, Bible study is aimed at finding specific answers to specific needs, concerns, questions, or problems.

A person may have questions about why God acts in particular ways. A person may question why God fails to act in a particular situation in the way we desire or think He should. A person may have questions about what God wants him to do, which decision he should make, or which path he should follow. These questions should motivate a person to go to his Bible to study what God says on the matter. An honest question is always an excellent beginning point for Bible study!

The apostle Paul wrote to Timothy:

> Be diligent to present yourself approved to God, a worker who does not need to be ashamed, rightly dividing the word of truth.

> —2 Timothy 2:15

To "rightly divide" the word of truth means to see the *whole* of God's truth and to separate from the truth anything that might be a lie. It is a sifting process, taking out anything that might pollute or detract from the truth. Bible study helps us to refine our understanding of God's Word.

In the refinement of metals such as silver and gold, the metal is heated to an extremely high temperature and is brought to a liquid state. The lighter impurities in the metal float to the top of the liquid and are skimmed off. The heavier and more valuable metal remains at the bottom. That is what happens when we engage in a diligent study of God's Word on a particular matter. We come to an understanding that is clearer, purer, and more concentrated. We truly *know* what God has to say on a matter.

Be diligent to present yourself approved to God, a worker who does not need to be ashamed, rightly dividing the word of truth.

—2 Timothy 2:15

What does it mean to be "rightly dividing the word of truth"? How is this done? What is your role in the process? What is God's role?

Why does Paul command us to "be diligent" in this matter? Why is diligence necessary?

Today and Tomorrow

TODAY: GOD REVEALS HIMSELF CLEARLY TO HIS PEOPLE THROUGH HIS WORD, THE BIBLE.

TOMORROW: I WILL BEGIN A DAILY HABIT OF READING THE BIBLE THIS WEEK.

LESSON 5

Getting to Know the Lord

──────── 🕭 **In This Lesson** 🕭 ────────

LEARNING: WHAT IS THE PURPOSE OF PRAYER?

GROWING: HOW AM I SUPPOSED TO PRAY—FOR MYSELF AND OTHERS?

──────── ⌘ ────────

There is only one way to develop a deep friendship and that is to spend time with a person, sharing mutual experiences as well as communicating ideas, dreams, hopes, and beliefs. Spending time together, sharing experiences, talking things over—these basic ingredients for developing a relationship with another human being are the same basic ingredients for developing a relationship with God.

Are you aware that we are commanded to pray? Jesus said to His disciples, "Watch and pray, lest you enter into temptation. The spirit indeed is willing, but the flesh is weak" (Matt. 26:41). Prayer is not just a good idea, it's God's command. It is a requirement if we are to become and remain strong in the Lord and develop an intimate relationship with Him.

Seven Aspects of an Effective Prayer Life

There are at least seven specific aspects of prayer that we should consider as we seek to become spiritually disciplined and to grow spiritually.

1. Continual Prayer

We are called to *pray continually*. Many Christians pray only in church. Some say grace at mealtimes, others say bedtime prayers with their children. All of these are appropriate times to pray, but the command to Christians from God's Word is to "pray without ceasing" (1 Thess. 5:17). We pray at all times, without ceasing, by living in an attitude of prayer.

To pray is to communicate with God, which includes both talking to and listening to God. Prayer includes both praise and thanksgiving. To pray without ceasing is to talk to God about virtually everything and to feel free to do so at any time and in any place. It is to discuss with God any problem or need that you face. It is to praise or thank God immediately when good things come your way. It is to converse with Him about decisions you must make, circumstances that require your involvement, and issues you must resolve. It is to be constantly on the alert to see what God wants you to see and to have spiritual ears open to hear what God wants you to hear.

Through the centuries God's people developed a habit of praying morning, noon, and night. Prayer was not limited to these times but was offered as a community at these times every day. I know of no better way to start a day and end a day than in prayer. The greatest way to frame a day is to frame it in prayer—seeking God's guidance, protection, and wisdom for the coming day as you pray in the morning and thanking God for His abundant provision to you as you prepare to sleep in the evening.

I believe that God is pleased when you set aside specific times to pray. To do so is to make prayer an intentional part of your life; it is to develop the *habit* of prayer, which is one of the most beneficial habits you can ever develop. It is to say to God, to yourself, and to others, "I value my relationship with God, and I am setting aside a part of every day just to be with Him and to talk things over with Him."

Confess your trespasses to one another, and pray for one another, that you may be healed. The effective, fervent prayer of a righteous man avails much.

—James 5:16

🖎 Why are we commanded to confess our sins to one another, as well as to God? What does this have to do with healing?

🖎 What is "fervent prayer"? How is it different from other forms of prayer?

2. Petitioning for Our Needs

We are to pray for God to meet our needs, including our need for forgiveness. It is not self-centered for you to pray for yourself, your family, or your loved ones. God wants you to pray for your own needs! The nature of the need may be physical, financial, emotional, or spiritual—no need is too small or too great to take to God. A part of our prayer every day should be a prayer confessing our sins and asking God to forgive us, cleanse us, and help us make the necessary changes in our lives so that we do not keep repeating sin.

3. Praise and Thanksgiving

We are to accompany our petitions with praise and thanksgiving. Paul urged the early church to pray without ceasing: "Rejoice always, pray without ceasing, in everything give thanks; for this is the will of God in Christ Jesus for you" (1 Thess. 5:16–18).

First, rejoice. Give praise. Be grateful that you have a relationship with the Lord. Praise Him for His wonderful deeds. Praise Him for all that He is, and all that He has done, including the specific things He has done and will do in your life.

Second, make your petitions. Tell God your concerns and needs. And third, give thanks that God is already working on your behalf to cause *all* things to be used for your eternal good (Rom. 8:28). Our prayers take on a much different tone and character when we begin them with praise and end them with thanksgiving!

When Jesus gave His model prayer to His disciples, He began it with words of praise: "Our Father in heaven, hallowed be Your name" (Matt. 6:9). To hallow the Lord's name is to declare it holy and worthy to be lifted higher than any other name. When we say, "Hallowed be Your name," we are praising the name of the Lord, exalting Him to a position of absolute supremacy.

Look also at how the Lord ended His model prayer: "For Yours is the kingdom and the power and the glory forever" (Matt. 6:13). He ended the prayer with praise and thanksgiving. The overall model of the Lord's Prayer is praise, petition, praise.

> Be anxious for nothing, but in everything by prayer and supplication, with thanksgiving, let your requests be made known to God.

> —Philippians 4:6

🙠 Why does Paul command us not to be anxious? How does anxiety hinder prayer? What part does your free will play in dealing with anxiety?

🙠 What is the difference between prayer and supplication? Why are we commanded to add thanksgiving into that combination?

4. An Attitude of Forgiveness

We are to pray with an attitude of forgiveness toward others. The Bible makes it very clear that, unless we forgive others, we cannot receive God's forgiveness. Our unforgiving attitude acts as a barrier, keeping us from receiving the fullness of what God desires to give us. Jesus taught, "If you forgive men their trespasses, your heavenly Father will also forgive you. But if you do not forgive men their trespasses, neither will your Father forgive your trespasses" (Matt. 6:14–15).

☙ Why does God not forgive us when we refuse to forgive others?

☙ Is there anyone in your life that you have not forgiven? How might this be preventing God's forgiveness in your own life?

5. Praying Without Doubt

We are to pray without doubting and without losing heart. James said this in his teaching that we are to ask God for wisdom: "Let him ask in faith, with no doubting, for he who doubts is like a wave of the sea driven and tossed by the wind. For let not that man suppose that he will receive anything from the Lord; he is a double-minded man, unstable in all his ways" (James 1:6–8). This is true in our prayers for wisdom, and in *all* our prayers.

Jesus taught, "Assuredly, I say to you, if you have faith and do not doubt ... also if you say to this mountain, 'Be removed and be cast into the sea,' it will be done. And whatever things you ask in prayer, believing, you will receive" (Matt. 21:21–22). To pray without doubt and without losing heart is to pray with *faith*. At all times our prayers must be steeped in faith if they are to be effective.

Why does James use the image of a wave to describe a person who lacks faith?

In what ways is a "double-minded man" unstable? How does faith bring stability?

6. Praying for Our Leaders

We are admonished in God's Word to pray for those in leadership over us. We should pray that those in authority will make decisions that allow us to live in peace and to freely share the gospel. Christians around the world are able to prosper spiritually under all kinds of governments, especially if the leader of the government allows religious freedom and freedom to share the gospel. Christians are able to work in any kind of environment, even slavery, and prosper spiritually, especially if the "boss" allows expressions of faith and opportunities for time off to worship with other believers.

A prayer for leaders should be that you and other Christians will be allowed to live in an environment that is conducive to godliness and reverence. The apostle Paul taught:

> Therefore I exhort first of all that supplications, prayers, intercessions, and giving of thanks be made for all men, for kings and all who are in authority, that we may lead a quiet and peaceable life in all godliness and reverence. For this is good and acceptable in the sight of God our Savior, who desires all men to be saved and to come to the knowledge of the truth.
>
> —1 Timothy 2:1–2

What is the reason for praying for our leaders, according to these verses?

🖎 Take time right now to pray for those in authority over you—employers, political leaders, church leaders, and others.

7. Intercession for Others

We are to ask for the prayers of others and offer prayers for others in need. God desires that we be in a giving and receiving relationship with others and that, as the body of Christ, we mutually bear one another's burdens. The disciples of Jesus were quick to ask for prayer and to offer prayer for others in need.

Peter and John were detained by Jewish authorities for healing a man in the name of Jesus and were later released with threats never to speak again in His name. They went immediately to their companions and reported what had happened, and the group responded with prayer: "They raised their voice to God with one accord" and prayed, "Lord, look on their threats, and grant to Your servants that with all boldness they may speak Your word, by stretching out Your hand to heal, and that signs and wonders may be done through the name of Your holy Servant Jesus" (Acts 4:24, 29–30). If Peter and John needed the prayers of others, how much more so do each of us need the prayers of fellow believers in Christ Jesus?

If you ever question what to pray for another Christian, let me suggest Paul's prayer for the Colossians below. It covers many of the basics that we know with certainty are the will of God for every person.

For this reason we also, since the day we heard it, do not cease to pray for you, and to ask that you may be filled with the knowledge of His will in all wisdom and spiritual understanding; that you may walk worthy of the Lord, fully pleasing Him, being fruitful in every good work and increasing in the knowledge of God; strengthened with all might, according to His glorious power, for all patience and longsuffering with joy; giving thanks to the Father who has qualified us to be partakers of the inheritance of the saints in the light.

—Colossians 1:9–12

☙ List below the specific things that Paul prays for others in these verses. Then define, in practical terms, what each means.

The person who prays daily and regularly with faith, perseverance, praise, and thanksgiving can expect answers from God! He can expect God to move obstacles and change situations and bring forth blessings. He can expect to experience a deepening intimacy in his relationship with the Lord. He can expect to grow spiritually and to be strong in faith. God hears our prayers. He answers them for our eternal benefit. And He invites us to an ever-deepening relationship with Him.

I desire therefore that the men pray everywhere, lifting up holy hands, without wrath and doubting.

—1 Timothy 2:8

~ What does it mean to lift up holy hands? What happens to our prayers if we lift up unholy hands?

~ How can wrath hinder our prayers? How might wrath and doubting be related?

❧ Today and Tomorrow ❧

TODAY: PRAYER IS A VITAL PART OF GROWING IN CHRIST—PRAYER FOR MYSELF AND FOR OTHERS.

TOMORROW: I WILL ADD REGULAR PRAYER TO MY DAILY SCHEDULE OF BIBLE-READING THIS WEEK.

❧ Notes and Prayer Requests: ❧

LESSON 6

Looking for Christ in All Things

┌─────────────── ᔥ **In This Lesson** ᔥ ───────────────┐

LEARNING: DOES GOD SPEAK TO US IN WAYS BESIDES THE BIBLE?

GROWING: HOW CAN I LEARN TO HEAR HIS VOICE?

└───────────────────── ∞ ─────────────────────┘

In the last chapter, we briefly touched upon the fact that listening is an integral part of all communication, including our communication with God. Listening involves far more than simply waiting for God to reply to our prayers. It involves an active listening—an intent watching and waiting anticipation—for God to speak to us continually. Listening is to be our attitude toward the Lord always. We are to expect the Lord to speak to us and should keep our hearts and minds open to Him so He might speak by any means at any time. To listen in this way is to be available to the Lord without hindrance.

Our attitudes are mental and emotional habits. Like all other habits, we can practice them and develop them over time. You can *choose* what you will think about and how you will respond to life. The more you make positive, godly choices in your thought life, the more likely those choices are going to be your *habitual responses* in times of crisis or deep need.

Four Ways to Develop an Attitude of Listening

There are four key things we can do to discipline ourselves into developing this habit of listening and of being available to the Lord always:

1. Wait in God's Presence

Set aside times to wait upon the Lord in silence. So often we spend our prayer time talking to the Lord without spending any time just waiting in silence to see what the Lord might say to us. Take time to sit or kneel in silence before the Lord. Empty your mind of all other thoughts. Concentrate on His Word and His presence with you. Ask Him to speak to you.

Many people today seem to be uncomfortable with silence, especially if they are alone. It is in silence, however, that we are able to hear the "still, small voice" of the Lord. Certainly the prophet Elijah knew this. After receiving a death threat from Queen Jezebel, Elijah escaped to an isolated desert area. There, in a cave, he heard the Lord say to him:

> "Go out, and stand on the mountain before the LORD." And behold, the LORD passed by, and a great and strong wind tore into the mountains and broke the rocks in pieces before the LORD, but the LORD was not in the wind; and after the wind an earthquake, but the LORD was not in the earthquake; and after the earthquake a fire, but the LORD was not in the fire; and after the fire a still small voice. So it was, when Elijah heard it, that he wrapped his face in his mantle and went out and stood in the entrance of the cave. Suddenly a voice came to him, and said, "What are you doing here, Elijah?"
>
> —1 Kings 19:11–13

What was God teaching Elijah by contrasting the mighty wind, earthquake, and fire with the still, small voice?

What does this teach concerning prayer?

2. Practice Frequent Praise

Praise the Lord often, regardless of your circumstances. Many people only praise the Lord when something good happens to them or when they receive an unexpected blessing. The Lord is worthy of our praise at *all* times, in *all* circumstances. We do not praise the Lord on the basis of circumstances; we praise the Lord on the basis of *who He is* in the midst of the circumstances. We do not praise the Lord because of the way we *feel* but because of *who He is* and the way He feels about us!

Don't limit your praise to the song service at church. Praise the Lord often, in both words and songs that you create spontaneously. All around you, at all times, you can find countless things for which to praise the Lord. Look for those things and voice your praise and thanksgiving to God.

When you are alone in your car, alone in an elevator, alone in your office, or alone in your home, take that opportunity to voice praise to the Lord for who He is, what He has done through the ages, what He has done in your life and in the lives of your loved ones, and what He is doing for you now and will do for you throughout all eternity. You can never run out of things for which to praise God.

When you voice praise to the Lord, you will experience the presence of God with you. The Bible tells us that the Lord is enthroned in the praises of His people (Ps. 22:3). The greater your praise, the smaller your problems are likely to appear. The more frequent your praise, the less you will find yourself with time to worry or feel anxious. The more you praise the Lord, the more you are going to see things that are worthy of His praise. Your entire attitude will shift from being me-centered and problem-centered to being God-centered and answer-centered.

O LORD, You are my God. I will exalt You, I will praise Your name, for You have done wonderful things; Your counsels of old are faithfulness and truth.

—Isaiah 25:1

Spend some time right now praising God for what He has done on your behalf—past, present, and future.

3. See Christ in All Things

Look for evidence of Christ in every circumstance. In even the worst disaster or most overwhelming crisis, Christ is present. When we find ourselves confused, frustrated, or overwhelmed by situations around us, the best question we can ask is, "Father, what do You want to do in this situation?" Asking that question immediately shifts your focus off the problem and onto the One who has all the answers and provision in His hand.

The Lord is utterly faithful, and He is with us *always*. There is no moment of any day of your life that He is beyond hearing your heart's cry or your sincere question. How and when the Lord chooses to speak to you of His purposes is up to the Lord. We cannot force the Lord to answer us *when* we desire an answer or *in the way* we desire. The person who asks a question of the Lord with a sincere desire for understanding, however, is going to receive an answer from the Lord in His timing and by His methods. Listen for it!

If then you were raised with Christ, seek those things which are above, where Christ is, sitting at the right hand of God. Set your mind on things above, not on things on the earth.

—Colossians 3:1–2

What does it mean to "set your mind on things above"? How is this done, in practical terms?

How does such a mind-set influence our prayers? Our overall attitude? Our reactions to life's surprises?

4. Listen for Opportunities to Give a Witness

Look and listen continually for opportunities to witness to Christ. Every conversation you have with a friend or coworker, every encounter you have with a stranger, every chance meeting is a potential opportunity to share a word about God's love. Many people think that to give a witness for the Lord is limited to explaining the plan of salvation. Many times our witness to another person is a reminder of God's love, a word of wisdom from God's Word, or a word of encouragement. Look for ways continually to insert the name of Jesus into your conversations. At times, the Lord may want us to admonish or to pray for a person. All of those are ways of witnessing to a person that God cares, God loves, God forgives, and God is present.

Ask the Lord as you prepare to meet with a person who is sick, in need, or just stopping by for a friendly visit, "What would *You* say to this person if You were meeting with him today?" Listen for the Lord's answer.

> But sanctify the Lord God in your hearts, and always be ready to give a defense to everyone who asks you a reason for the hope that is in you, with meekness and fear; having a good conscience, that when they defame you as evildoers, those who revile your good conduct in Christ may be ashamed.
>
> —1 Peter 3:15–16

☙ What does it mean to "sanctify the Lord God in your hearts"? How does this influence your prayers? Your responses to everyday life? To people around you?

☙ According to these verses, what is involved in witnessing to others about Christ?

Eyes to See and Ears to Hear

Jesus frequently called His disciples to have "eyes to see" and "ears to hear" what God was desiring to do in their midst (Matt. 11:15; 13:9, for example). Those who had ears to hear both heard and understood what the Lord was telling them. That is the goal for all of our listening: a greater understanding of what the Lord is desiring to communicate to us and through us. We are developing eyes to see and ears to hear when we spend time listening to the Lord, praise Him frequently, look continually for His presence and work in our midst, and look continually for opportunities to give witness to Him.

❧ Today and Tomorrow ☙

TODAY: GOD DOES SPEAK TO ME—BUT I MUST FIRST BE WILLING TO LISTEN.

TOMORROW: I WILL PRACTICE LISTENING IN SILENCE DURING MY PRAYER TIMES THIS WEEK.

❧ Notes and Prayer Requests: ❧

∽∞∽ **Notes and Prayer Requests:** ∽∞∽

LESSON 7

Faithful Giving

─────── ❧ **In This Lesson** ❦ ───────

LEARNING: WHAT IS THE REASON FOR TITHING?

GROWING: WHAT IS CONSIDERED A "CORRECT" TITHE?

──────── ✷ ────────

The Christian life is intended to be a life of generous giving. One of the most blessed and rewarding aspects of spiritual discipline is giving regularly of one's time, talents, and material substance. The basic understanding of all believers in Christ Jesus is that everything we have received in this life is a gift to us from God: every minute that we live, every ability we possess, every opportunity we are given, every child that we bear, every item of material wealth, and even our abilities to express love and have faith. God gives to us first, and it is out of the abundance of His supply to us that we give.

> Now therefore, our God, we thank You and praise Your glorious name. But who am I, and who are my people, that we should be able to offer so willingly as this? For all things come from You, and of Your own we have given You.
>
> —1 Chronicles 29:13–14

∾ What is the writer of these verses suggesting about the gifts that God's people offer to Him as sacrifices?

∾ According to these verses, where do all blessings originate? What does this suggest about our obligation to give tithes?

Three Attributes of Our Giving

God gives to us first, and He is the Source of all that we have in life. The Lord challenges us to three very specific ways of expressing our faith through giving.

1. Cheerful Giving

We are to be cheerful givers. Too often, Christians have a negative reaction to those who preach about giving. In all likelihood, they also have a negative reaction toward the act of giving! Giving, however, is commanded by God. Jesus taught, "Give, and it will be given to you" (Luke 6:38). He said, "Freely you have received, freely give" (Matt. 10:8). Giving is a means of activating our faith, meeting needs, and bringing about an abundant return. When we catch a glimpse of the great rewards associated with our giving, we cannot help but be cheerful!

We do not give to God in order to "pay God" for anything. God's gift of salvation to us is a free gift motivated by His unlimited love for us. The same is true for all of God's gifts to us: He gives to us because we are His beloved children. Rather, our giving to God allows God to meet our needs, to meet the needs of others, and to cause a great abundance of joy and blessings to come our way. Jesus said that, when we give, what is returned to us will be in "good measure, pressed down, shaken together, and running over will be put into your bosom. For with the same measure that you use, it will be measured back to you" (Luke 6:38). God multiplies what we give in ways that we cannot understand, but in which we surely can receive!

> So let each one give as he purposes in his heart, not grudgingly or of necessity; for God loves a cheerful giver.
>
> —2 Corinthians 9:7

☙ When you give of your income to the Lord's work, what is your attitude? Do you tend to be grudging, or do you tithe cheerfully?

☙ Why does Paul command us to give as we "purpose in our heart"? Why does he not provide a formula for giving?

2. Consistent Giving

We are to be consistent givers. The standard that God sets for our giving is a tithe of what we receive, a tithe being one-tenth. Our giving is not to be sporadic or scattered, but consistent and focused. As we receive, we are to give a tenth to God's work—regularly. We are to give to the place where we participate in the worship of the Lord—the tithe is not intended for a charitable organization but for a work that bears the Lord's name. It is to further the work of the Lord, which is the spreading of the gospel and the teaching of God's Word.

Read this passage from Malachi:

> "Will a man rob God?
> Yet you have robbed Me!
> But you say,
> 'In what way have we robbed You?'
> In tithes and offerings.
> You are cursed with a curse,
> For you have robbed Me,
> Even this whole nation.
> Bring all the tithes into the storehouse,
> That there may be food in My house,
> And try Me now in this,"
> Says the LORD of hosts,
> "If I will not open for you the windows of heaven
> And pour out for you such blessing
> That there will not be room enough to receive it.
> And I will rebuke the devourer for your sakes,
> So that he will not destroy the fruit of your ground,
> Nor shall the vine fail to bear fruit for you in the field,"
> Says the LORD of hosts;
> "And all nations will call you blessed,

For you will be a delightful land,"
Says the Lord of hosts.

—Malachi 3:8–12

☙ According to these verses, what is God's view of a person who fails to tithe?

☙ What are the results of consistently giving back to God?

God draws a very clear line. Those who fail to give according to His commandment are not blessed, while those who do give tithes and offerings *are* blessed.

There are Christians who believe that tithing was only for Old Testament times. Why didn't Jesus teach about tithing? Because the people were already tithing! Tithing was deeply ingrained in the fabric of the society in which Jesus ministered. There was no reason to preach about something the people were already doing. In fact, the deeply religious Pharisees were tithing the herbs that grew in their gardens. Jesus did not criticize their tithing; instead, He approved of their tithing and said that they were to place greater importance on bigger issues: God's justice and God's love.

He said, "You tithe mint and rue and all manner of herbs, and pass by justice and the love of God. These you ought to have done, without leaving the others undone" (Luke 11:42). Jesus also taught a great deal about giving to the needy (Matt. 25:37–40), and He taught sacrificial giving (Mark 12:41–44).

3. Generous Giving

We are to be generous givers. The first-century Christians were generous givers. They tithed to the storehouse of the Lord, and in some cases they sacrificed all they had for the benefit of their brothers and sisters in Christ (Acts 4:34–37).

The apostle Paul described a ministry gift of giving and admonished those with this gift to give "with liberality" (Rom. 12:8). Those who are called to such a ministry go beyond the giving of tithes and offerings. All of us, however, are challenged to give with generosity: to go above and beyond the tithe and give generous offerings. The degree to which we give is the degree to which we receive.

But this I say: He who sows sparingly will also reap sparingly, and he who sows bountifully will also reap bountifully.

—2 Corinthians 9:6

How is tithing similar to sowing seed in a garden?

What is the spirit of generous giving as described in this verse? What determines God's blessing: the amount given or the spirit of the giver?

An Expression of Trust in God

Our giving is a direct expression of our trust in God. It is a sign of our willingness to let go of the controls of our life and our material well-being and let God direct us, use us, and bless us as He desires. The psalmist wrote:

> Oh, taste and see that the Lord is good;
> Blessed is the man who trusts in Him!
> Oh, fear the Lord, you His saints!
> There is no want to those who fear Him.
> The young lions lack and suffer hunger;
> But those who seek the Lord shall not lack any good thing.

—Psalm 34:8–10

The promise of God to you as His beloved child is that He "shall supply all your need according to His riches in glory by Christ Jesus" (Phil. 4:19). Are you willing to trust God today with your giving? Are you willing to trust Him to take care of you and to meet all of your material needs? It takes discipline of your will to become a cheerful, consistent, and generous giver. Your giving is a key, however, to releasing the blessings of God into your life. It is vitally linked to your ability to trust God and to your ability to grow spiritually.

> And let us not grow weary while doing good, for in due season we shall reap if we do not lose heart.

—Galatians 6:9

What might cause a person to "grow weary" or "lose heart" concerning giving? What can you do to guard against this?

What harvest do we reap when we give generously to the Lord? Who is responsible for that harvest? For our giving?

Today and Tomorrow

TODAY: THE LORD WANTS ME TO GIVE BACK TO HIM SOME OF THE BLESS-INGS HE HAS GIVEN ME.

TOMORROW: I WILL BEGIN A REGULAR SCHEDULE OF TITHING THIS MONTH AND WILL WORK ON DOING IT CHEERFULLY.

Lesson 8

Involvement with Other Believers

In This Lesson

Learning: Is it really that important to go to church?

Growing: What difference can I make in a local church?

One of the most important spiritual disciplines you can develop is faithful involvement with other believers. I am always amazed when a Christian tells me, "Oh, I don't go to church very often. I'd rather stay at home and listen to Christian television or radio programs, or listen to Bible-teaching tapes." Others reluctantly admit to me, "We only go to church when we can work it into our family schedule" or "I go to church *as often as I can,*" which usually means not very often.

I certainly am all in favor of Christian television, radio, and tape ministries, but I also know they are no substitute for your regular attendance and faithful involvement in the worship services, ministry outreaches, and educational programs of your church. The writer to the Hebrews said:

> Let us consider one another in order to stir up love and good works, not forsaking the assembling of ourselves together, as is the manner of some, but exhorting one another, and so much the more as you see the Day approaching.
>
> —Hebrews 10:24–25

∾ What does it mean to "stir up love and good works"? Why do such things need to be stirred up?

∾ Why is it necessary that other Christians be involved in that process? What role does the church play, according to these verses?

The Body of Christ

No Christian has ever been called to "go it alone" in his or her faith. We need one another. The church was designed from the beginning to function as the living body of Christ on the earth after the Lord's resurrection and ascension. The apostle Paul wrote:

For as we have many members in one body, but all the members do not have the same function, so we, being many, are one body in Christ, and individually members of one another. Having then gifts differing according to the grace that is given to us, let us use them: if prophecy, let us prophesy in proportion to our faith; or ministry, let us use it in our ministering; he who teaches, in teaching; he who exhorts, in exhortation; he who gives, with liberality; he who leads, with diligence; he who shows mercy, with cheerfulness.

—Romans 12:4–8

Part of the reason that we need to be in regular fellowship with other believers is so that we might receive the benefit of their spiritual gifts and, in turn, give our spiritual gifts to the body of Christ. We individually are made stronger as we both receive and give. Simultaneously, the church to which we belong is made stronger and more effective as a whole.

Why does Paul use the analogy of the human body to describe the church? How does this illustrate the importance of regular church involvement?

What is the purpose of spiritual gifts, according to the passage above? Where are they to be used?

Our Ministry to Other Believers

Jesus made it very clear that our foremost ministry to other believers is to love them. He said to His disciples shortly before His crucifixion: "This is My commandment, that you love one another as I have loved you" (John 15:12). The apostle Paul echoed this command: "Be imitators of God as dear children. And walk in love, as Christ also has loved us and given Himself for us" (Eph. 5:1–2).

The New Testament writers identified several specific ways in which we are called to show love to one another within the body of Christ. Paul wrote to the Colossians:

> Let the peace of God rule in your hearts, to which also you were called in one body; and be thankful. Let the word of Christ dwell in you richly in all wisdom, teaching and admonishing one another in psalms and hymns and spiritual songs, singing with grace in your hearts to the Lord. And whatever you do in word or deed, do all in the name of the Lord Jesus, giving thanks to God the Father through Him.
>
> —Colossians 3:15–17

As members of the Body of Christ, we are to

 pray for one another (James 5:16).

 speak well of one another (James 4:11).

 speak truthful and admonishing words to one another (Rom. 15:14).

 be hospitable and giving to one another (1 Peter 4:9–10).

☙ comfort one another (1 Thess. 5:11).

☙ pursue the common good (1 Thess. 5:15).

☙ encourage and build up one another (1 Cor. 14:26).

☙ bless one another (1 Peter 3:8–9).

☙ List the functions of the church, in your own words, from each passage below.

Romans 15:14

1 Corinthians 14:26

1 Thessalonians 5:11, 15

James 4:11

James 5:16

1 Peter 4:9–10

Our Service to Others Outside the Church

Along with others in the body of Christ, we are to be involved in active ministry to those who do not know the Lord. Jesus sent out His disciples two by two. He gave them power and authority over all demons and power to cure diseases. He told them to preach the kingdom of God and heal the sick (Luke 9:1–2).

On another occasion Jesus sent out seventy of His disciples, again two by two, and He said to them, "The harvest truly is great, but the laborers are few; therefore pray the Lord of the harvest to send out laborers into His harvest ... Heal the sick there, and say to them, 'The kingdom of God has come near to you' " (Luke 10:2, 9).

If we desire to be followers of Jesus today, we must acknowledge that He is sending us out as well. He is saying the same things to us: we are to heal the sick and proclaim the kingdom of God.

Taking On the Ministry of Christ

Jesus used the words of Isaiah to describe His ministry on earth:

The Spirit of the Lord GOD is upon Me,
Because the LORD has anointed Me
To preach good tidings to the poor;
He has sent Me to heal the brokenhearted,
To proclaim liberty to the captives,
And the opening of the prison to those who are bound;
To proclaim the acceptable year of the Lord,
And the day of vengeance of our God;
To comfort all who mourn,
To console those who mourn in Zion,

To give them beauty for ashes,
The oil of joy for mourning,
The garment of praise for the spirit of heaviness;
That they may be called trees of righteousness,
The planting of the Lord, that He may be glorified.

—Isaiah 61:1–3

❧ What roles of the church does Jesus describe in these verses?

❧ Which of those roles are you involved with? Which of those ministries have you been a recipient of?

Jesus also taught His disciples:

> Then the King will say to those on His right hand, "Come, you blessed of My Father, inherit the kingdom prepared for you from the foundation of the world: for I was hungry and you gave Me food; I was thirsty and you gave Me drink; I was a stranger and you took Me in; I was naked and you clothed Me; I was sick and you visited Me; I was in prison and you came to Me." Then the righteous will answer Him, saying, "Lord, when did we see You hungry and feed You, or thirsty and give You drink? When did we see You a stranger and take You in, or naked and clothe You? Or when did we see You sick, or in prison, and come to You?" And the King will answer and say to them, "Assuredly, I say to you, inasmuch as you did it to one of the least of these My brethren, you did it to Me."
>
> —Matthew 25:34–40

⇜ What roles of the church does Jesus describe in this parable?

⇜ Why does Jesus say that we are ministering to Him when we minister to other people? What does this imply concerning your involvement in a local church?

We are never called to "go it alone" in our faith, and we are never called to "go it alone" in ministry to others. Jesus sent out His disciples *two by two*. He said, "If two of you agree on earth concerning anything that they ask, it will be done for them by My Father in heaven. For where two or three are gathered together in My name, I am there in the midst of them" (Matt. 18:19–20).

Paul encouraged the Philippians, "Stand fast in one spirit, with one mind striving together for the faith of the gospel" (Phil. 1:27). In Revelation, John recorded again and again these four convicting words of Jesus: "I know your works" (Rev. 2:2, 9, 19, for example). What we do as the body of Christ—as unto the Lord, unto one another, and unto the lost—is the basis on which we will be judged and rewarded.

> ...that there should be no schism in the body, but that the members should have the same care for one another. And if one member suffers, all the members suffer with it; or if one member is honored, all the members rejoice with it. Now you are the body of Christ, and members individually.
>
> —1 Corinthians 12:25–27

☙ When have you experienced pain in a small part of your body, such as a stubbed toe? How did you react to that pain?

Why is it important for all Christians to be involved regularly with a local church, according to these verses? What happens when one part of the body becomes separated?

Today and Tomorrow

TODAY: I AM PART OF CHRIST'S BODY, AND THEREFORE I MUST REMAIN CONNECTED TO OTHER PARTS OF HIS BODY.

TOMORROW: I WILL BECOME INVOLVED IN THE MINISTRIES OF A LOCAL CHURCH ON A REGULAR BASIS.

LESSON 9

The Four R's of Spiritual Growth

──────── ✎ **In This Lesson** ✍ ────────

LEARNING: IF GOD LOVES ME, WHY DO I HAVE TO SUFFER?

GROWING: HOW CAN I LEARN FROM THOSE WHO ARE WISE?

⌘

Are you aware that Christians are *commanded* to grow spiritually? We are commanded to practice spiritual disciplines and to mature. Peter said, "Grow in the grace and knowledge of our Lord and Savior Jesus Christ" (2 Peter 3:18). This is not a nice statement of encouragement or advice: it is a command from the Lord.

None of us automatically grows spiritually. Each of us must choose to grow. And we must choose to *continue* to grow. We must never be satisfied with our current level of spiritual strength. We must always seek to become stronger, more mature, and more effective for the Lord. In God's Word we find four keys that are prerequisites to growth, no matter how mature a person may be in the Lord.

1. Ready to Face Failures

Most of us try to dismiss, sidestep, or justify our faults and failures. We sometimes try to take the easy way out, saying, "That's just the way I am" or "That's the way I was raised." The fact is, most of us are not just the way that God wants us to be. Before the basic spiritual disciplines can be effective, maturing us into the likeness of Christ Jesus, we must face our faults and failures, take responsibility for them, and go to God with them.

Is there an area in your life where you have experienced repeated failures? Can you point to certain faults that you seem to have had all your life? Let me assure you, God has a way for those failures to be turned into victories and strengths. God has a great desire to see you made whole, and He will continue to pursue the faults and failures that fragment you and cause you to be dysfunctional, uneasy, or deeply frustrated. He will continue to move against any obstacle that stands in the way of your wholeness or intimacy with Him.

The first step is one that we must take: own up to our failures, flaws, and faults. Stop blaming others and assume responsibility. Confess to God, "I have brought myself to the place where I am today." Admit, "I am the one who has allowed this past to continue to be my present."

True repentance is moving in the opposite direction from past sin. It is an act of the will, empowered by the Holy Spirit within us, to change from our wicked ways, evil attitudes, hurtful words, and wrong behaviors. For a person to repent he first must own up to those things that need to be changed. If the spiritual disciplines you practice are going to be effective, you must recognize that some things about your life need healing and that you are responsible for using your will and faith to bring about changes.

Therefore we also, since we are surrounded by so great a cloud of witnesses, let us lay aside every weight, and the sin which so easily ensnares us, and let us run with endurance the race that is set before us.

—Hebrews 12:1

❧ What is the race that has been "set before" you? In what areas do you need more endurance?

❧ What sins frequently ensnare you? What weights are slowing you down? What will you do this week to get rid of these things?

2. Receive Godly Counsel

Every Christian, no matter his degree of spiritual strength and maturity, can benefit from wise counsel that is couched in love, forgiveness, and confidentiality. God has placed Christian brothers and sisters in your life to encourage you, to admonish you, to teach you, and to give you godly counsel regarding God's unique plan and purpose for your life. Avail yourself of their help!

In order to benefit from wise counsel, a person must choose to be transparent and vulnerable emotionally. He must choose to be candid, forthcoming, and truthful about his own life, desires, and motivations. He must face up to the fact that he does not know fully all that God wants him to know and that he needs the greater wisdom that can come only as we share our life in Christ.

The Word of God is always the basis for wise counsel. All advice that we receive must flow from God's Word and be echoed by God's Word. If you truly desire to grow to full spiritual maturity in Christ Jesus, you need to avail yourself of the wisdom others can offer to you.

> So then, my beloved brethren, let every man be swift to hear, slow to speak, slow to wrath; for the wrath of man does not produce the righteousness of God.
>
> —James 1:19–20

⌘ What is involved in being "swift to hear"? Why must we be "slow to speak"?

⤶ What role does wrath play in one's willingness to hear wise counsel? How does man's wrath keep God's righteousness from being produced?

3. Reflect on God's Work

The Bible commands us to live a *daily* life, to trust God to meet our daily needs and to walk fully in the present moment of our existence. At the same time we find numerous instances in God's Word in which the people were called to reflect upon God's goodness to them, or to catch a glimpse of the broader, universal, and eternal work God is doing, both in the world today and throughout the ages.

It is as we learn about and study the ways in which God has worked in the lives of others that we gain a greater understanding of how God will work in our lives. We can learn a great deal by hearing and reflecting upon the way God is working in the lives of other Christians today, including those whom we recognize as more mature in Christ Jesus.

If you are to benefit fully from practicing spiritual disciplines, you need to be able to see your life in the broader context of what God is doing and what He desires to do in the world. You must see how your life meshes with the lives of others in your family, your church, and your community. You must gain an understanding that what the Lord desires to do *in* you is aimed at what He desires ultimately to do *through* you.

Now, therefore, you are no longer strangers and foreigners, but fellow citizens with the saints and members of the household of God, having been built on the foundation of the apostles and prophets, Jesus Christ Himself being the chief cornerstone, in whom the whole building, being fitted together, grows into a holy temple in the Lord, in whom you also are being built together for a dwelling place of God in the Spirit.

—Ephesians 2:19–22

Put these verses into your own words. What principle is Paul addressing here?

How do these verses demonstrate that all Christians can learn from God's involvement in the lives of other Christians? In what ways are you blessed by God's work in those who have gone before?

4. Response to Trials

The person who practices spiritual disciplines and is growing in Christ Jesus must recognize that he is going to face trials and tests in life. Many people believe that God should spare a Christian from all negative experiences. In fact, God uses trials and tests for our benefit. They become our opportunity to learn more about God's methods, purposes, and perfect plan; they are our school for learning how to grow stronger in faith.

If you are practicing spiritual disciplines, you are going to be better equipped to face trials and tests that come your way. Rather than run from them, ask the Lord why He has allowed a specific trial or test to come into your life. Look for the lesson that He desires to teach you or the character trait He desires to strengthen. God knows all about the test you are experiencing, and He has allowed it to come into your life for a purpose. Ask Him to reveal that purpose to you. Ask Him to help you trust Him to bring you through the trial in a way that results in glory to Him.

At the same time ask the Lord if the trial you are experiencing is a chastening from Him. The Lord only chastens those whom He loves and desires to perfect. Ask the Lord, "Is there something in my life that You want me to change?" If the answer is yes, act quickly to obey the Lord's command or to confess the sin that is holding you back from spiritual growth.

> Beloved, do not think it strange concerning the fiery trial which is to try you, as though some strange thing happened to you; but rejoice to the extent that you partake of Christ's sufferings, that when His glory is revealed, you may also be glad with exceeding joy.

> —1 Peter 4:12–13

☙ When have you gone through a "fiery trial" which actually strengthened your character? What trials might God be using right now to make you more like Christ?

☙ What are we called to rejoice in when we face trials? How can such rejoicing actually make a trial more helpful?

We must never lose sight of the fact that we are in relationship with a *holy* God. God manifests no darkness, no shadow of turning, and no tolerance for evil or deceit. For us to approach God, we must be in a state of forgiveness, which is only made possible as we face up to our sin, seek God's forgiveness, and choose to live in His righteousness. This is a daily decision that each of us must make: a daily decision to confess our sin, a daily receiving of His forgiveness, and a daily desire to walk in the paths that the Holy Spirit reveals to us.

A person who refuses to face his failures and faults cannot grow spiritually. A person who refuses to receive godly counsel cannot grow into great spiritual maturity. A person who does not see his life in the broader context of God's plan for all mankind cannot know how to employ spiritual strength and power. A person who is unwilling to face life's trials and troubles with a reliance upon God cannot become strong spiritually. A person who is unwilling to be chastened by the Lord cannot grow into perfection in Christ Jesus.

Each of us must be willing to face our faults, confess our sins, receive godly counsel, seek God's "big picture" for our life, trust God regardless of circumstances, and yield to the chastening of the Lord if we are to benefit fully from the practice of spiritual disciplines. A Christian can read his Bible daily, communicate with the Lord often in prayer, attend church regularly, be involved in outreach ministry, and give faithfully, but unless he is willing to change, to grow, to be perfected, and then to be used however God desires, these disciplines will not yield their maximum benefit. A total submission of our life to God's remolding and remaking of us is required.

And you have forgotten the exhortation which speaks to you
as to sons: *"My son, do not despise the chastening of the Lord,*
nor be discouraged when you are rebuked by Him; for whom
the Lord loves He chastens, and scourges every son whom He
receives."

—Hebrews 12:5–6

🕮 What does it mean to be a son of God? What privileges does
that bring? What responsibilities?

🕮 What is a scourge? Why would God choose to use a scourge
on a son that He loves? What is His purpose for chastening
us?

❧ Today and Tomorrow ❧

TODAY: GOD USES OTHER CHRISTIANS AS WELL AS CIRCUMSTANCES TO MAKE ME MORE LIKE CHRIST.

TOMORROW: I WILL ASK THE LORD THIS WEEK TO TEACH ME THROUGH OTHER CHRISTIANS AND THROUGH LIFE'S CIRCUMSTANCES.

❧ Notes and Prayer Requests: ❧

Notes and Prayer Requests:

LESSON 10

Ten Hallmarks of Spiritual Strength

─────── ❧ In This Lesson ❧ ───────

LEARNING: WHAT DISTINGUISHES A MATURE CHRISTIAN FROM AN IMMA-
TURE CHRISTIAN?

GROWING: HOW CAN I TELL IF I'M MAKING PROGRESS?

────── ⋙ ──────

From my many years of pastoring, I have concluded that there are ten hallmarks or signs that routinely appear in those who are spiritually strong. As you read through these attributes and study them, I encourage you to evaluate your own life and to refrain from judging others. These attributes may not be present in a person in equal amounts, but these are the marks of a person who is spiritually healthy and mature. They are the attributes of a person who has grown to a deep level of intimacy with God and who routinely experiences God's presence and power in his life.

1. A Great Hunger for God

Those who are spiritually mature have a hunger for the things of God. This hunger is what has led them to develop spiritual disciplines and to mature in Christ Jesus. Those with a hunger for God are not content with knowing Him in an objective way as Creator, Savior, or almighty God. They desire to know Him as Lord, to develop an intimate relationship with the Lord, to know what the Lord desires of them, and to experience the Lord's presence on a daily basis. They want to know God in all His fullness—Father, Son, and Holy Spirit. They desire to recognize and respond immediately to the prompting of the Holy Spirit however He may lead them.

> As the deer pants for the water brooks, so pants my soul for You, O God. My soul thirsts for God, for the living God. When shall I come and appear before God?
>
> —Psalm 42:1–2

⤳ When have you experienced a deep thirst for God's presence? How did you satisfy that thirst?

⤳ Where does such a longing come from? How can a Christian develop an ongoing thirst for God?

2. A Desire to Know God's Truth

The spiritually mature person knows God's Word and continually applies it in his life. He knows what the Bible has to say, and he also knows the meaning of the Scriptures and considers God's Word to be the ultimate authority in helping him make decisions and eternally significant choices.

> Teach me, O Lord, the way of Your statutes, and I shall keep it to the end. Give me understanding, and I shall keep Your law; indeed, I shall observe it with my whole heart.
>
> —Psalm 119:33–34

What is God's role in spiritual growth, according to these verses? What is your role?

Why is an understanding of God's Word not enough to become like Christ? What more is needed?

3. No Tolerance for Evil

The spiritually mature person has no tolerance for evil in any form. He is able to discern evil and recognize sin, and he has an abhorrence for all that is contrary to God's goodness, grace, mercy, love, and forgiveness.

The spiritually mature Christian is not judgmental of people but of actions and words. Christians are called to judge deeds, to judge right from wrong (1 Peter 4:17). The mature Christian has a desire to remove himself as far as possible from activities and situations that give rise to sin.

> Beloved, do not believe every spirit, but test the spirits, whether they are of God; because many false prophets have gone out into the world. By this you know the Spirit of God: Every spirit that confesses that Jesus Christ has come in the flesh is of God, and every spirit that does not confess that Jesus Christ has come in the flesh is not of God. And this is the spirit of the Antichrist, which you have heard was coming, and is now already in the world.
>
> —1 John 4:1–3

What does it mean to "test the spirits"? How is this done?

✎ What are some examples of false teachings that are popular today? How do you know these to be false?

4. A Desire for God's Will to Be Done

The Bible teaches that we as believers are *in* this world, but we are not to be *of* this world. While living in the world we must abide by natural laws, live within the constraints of man-made laws, and provide for ourselves within the systems of this world. But we are not to have the same desires and lusts that the world exhibits. We are not to have the same dreams, goals, or hopes. Rather, we are to desire with our whole heart that God's will be done on this earth. As we pray in the Lord's Prayer, "Your kingdom come. Your will be done on earth as it is in heaven" (Matthew 6:10).

Do not love the world or the things in the world. If anyone loves the world, the love of the Father is not in him. For all that is in the world—the lust of the flesh, the lust of the eyes, and the pride of life—is not of the Father but is of the world.

—1 John 2:15–16

🖎 Why are love of the world and love of the Father mutually exclusive? Why can't a Christian love the world *and* the Father at the same time?

🖎 Define the following, and give examples of each.

Lust of the flesh:

Lust of the eyes:

Pride of life:

5. A Growing Love for Others

The spiritually strong person exhibits spiritual power and also great love. The mature Christian is able to express love and has a desire to extend love to an ever-widening circle of people. The mature Christian has little concern with appearances, status, or personal reputation. His foremost concern is with expressing God's love to the sinner and to any person in need. He has an ever-growing desire to reach out, to touch, to speak, to share, to listen, and to be used by God to shower His love on those who are hurting.

> If someone says, "I love God," and hates his brother, he is a liar; for he who does not love his brother whom he has seen, how can he love God whom he has not seen? And this commandment we have from Him: that he who loves God must love his brother also.
>
> —1 John 4:20–21

∾ Why is it impossible to love God and hate one's brother at the same time?

∾ When have you been unlovable in the past? How did God show His love for you, even in those times?

6. Quickness to Forgive

The spiritually strong person is quick to forgive those who offend, hurt, or reject him. He harbors no resentment and is quick to make apologies, to make amends, and to settle disputes peacefully. He does not compromise with evil or have a desire to be yoked with nonbelievers. The mature Christian, rather, has a desire to live in peace with others and to live free of bitterness and feelings of revenge.

> But love your enemies, do good, and lend, hoping for nothing in return; and your reward will be great, and you will be sons of the Most High. For He is kind to the unthankful and evil. Therefore be merciful, just as your Father also is merciful.

> —Luke 6:35–36

☙ When have you done good to someone and received evil in return? When have you lent something that you never got back?

☙ What should be the Christian's mind-set when doing good? How does this attitude make us more like Christ?

7. Quickness to Obey

When the spiritually mature person receives a command from the Holy Spirit, he is quick to act. When he feels a conviction of sin, he is quick to confess his sin, seek God's forgiveness, and change his ways. The mature Christian has a deep desire to do God's will. He longs to hear God speak to him, and when He does, he responds enthusiastically and immediately, with full effort given to whatever God commands.

> Therefore whoever hears these sayings of Mine, and does them, I will liken him to a wise man who built his house on the rock: and the rain descended, the floods came, and the winds blew and beat on that house; and it did not fall, for it was founded on the rock.
>
> —Matthew 7:24–25

In what ways is a house more secure if it is built on solid rock rather than on sand? How is this a picture of building your life on God's Word?

What two things are required for a person to build his life on God's Word? How are these steps carried out?

8. Great Faith

Every person has been given a measure of faith (Rom. 12:3). But not every believer has developed the same degree of faith. Faith is intended to be used, to be exercised, and the more a person uses his faith, the stronger it grows. The Bible speaks of varying degrees of faith—from little faith (Matt. 14:31) to great faith (Matt. 15:28). The mature believer is developing and using his faith with the goal of having *great* faith.

> But when [Peter] saw that the wind was boisterous, he was afraid; and beginning to sink he cried out, saying, "Lord, save me!" And immediately Jesus stretched out His hand and caught him, and said to him, "O you of little faith, why did you doubt?"

> —Matthew 14:30–31

⤙ Peter had been walking on the water in these verses. In what way was his faith too small? How might it have been greater?

⤙ How has your own faith grown over the years? What has caused it to grow stronger?

9. A Soft Heart

The spiritually strong person has a soft heart toward those in need. He is tender and sensitive to those who are hurting, and he desires to respond in ways that are appropriate and bring glory to God. He has a strong desire to see sinners receive Jesus Christ as their Savior. He has a commitment to help in whatever way he can to see that the practical, emotional, and spiritual needs of others are met.

> Rejoice with those who rejoice, and weep with those who weep. Be of the same mind toward one another. Do not set your mind on high things, but associate with the humble. Do not be wise in your own opinion.

> —Romans 12:15–16

What sort of people in your circle of friends would be considered "humble"? How often do you associate with such people?

When has someone rejoiced with you or wept with you? How did that compassion demonstrate the love of God to you?

10. Deep Love for God

The spiritually mature person has a deep and abiding love for God. He recognizes God as his loving, merciful, patient heavenly Father—a Father who can be trusted completely to provide, give wisdom, be present always, bestow blessings, and give unconditional love.

> There is no fear in love; but perfect love casts out fear, because fear involves torment. But he who fears has not been made perfect in love. We love Him because He first loved us.
>
> —1 John 4:18–19

What sort of love is based upon fear? When have you felt that sort of love toward God or toward another person?

How does God love us? What sort of love best mirrors His love?

The Basics Never Change

Every coach knows that when a team gets into trouble, that is not the time to introduce new plays or change the overall strategy. Rather, it's time to return to basics, to reinforce the tried-and-true drills and practices. The same is true spiritually. Through the ages Christians have known that when they practice basic spiritual disciplines—reading God's Word daily, praying often, giving faithfully, attending church regularly, staying active in outreach ministries—they are much more likely to:

∾ hear from God.

∾ experience God's love, joy, and peace.

∾ grow in the effective use of their talents.

∾ receive blessings beyond anything they had asked or imagined (Eph. 3:20).

We never grow beyond our need for the basics. They are the foundation on which all other aspects of our Christian life are built. They are the disciplines that need to become deeply ingrained habits in us.

In which area of spiritual discipline do you find yourself lacking? Make the development or renewal of that particular discipline a priority in your life without neglecting the other disciplines. Then see what God will do in you, through you, and for you. It is as we practice the basics—regularly, consistently, and with perseverance—that we grow and become strong in the Lord.

❧ Today and Tomorrow ❧

TODAY: TO BECOME A MATURE BELIEVER, I MUST ALWAYS BE WORKING ON THE BASIC AREAS OF DISCIPLINE.

TOMORROW: I WILL CONTINUE IN THE COMING WEEKS TO MAINTAIN THE DISCIPLINES WHICH I'VE BEGUN.

❧ Notes and Prayer Requests: ❧

∽ **Notes and Prayer Requests:** ∽

∽∾ **Notes and Prayer Requests:** ∽∾

⌘ Notes and Prayer Requests: ⌘

Notes and Prayer Requests:

∞ Notes and Prayer Requests: ∞

∞ Notes and Prayer Requests: ∞

⤨ Notes and Prayer Requests: ⤨

The Life Principles Series

STUDY GUIDES

Other Books by Charles Stanley